DUDLEY
THROUGH TIME
Peter Glews

AMBERLEY PUBLISHING

To Bill and Dot
My loving parents
Who never got my collecting bug

First published 2010

Amberley Publishing Plc
Cirencester Road, Chalford,
Stroud, Gloucestershire, GL6 8PE

www.amberley-books.com

Copyright © Peter Glews 2010

The right of Paul Hurley to be identified as the
Author of this work has been asserted in accordance
with the Copyrights, Designs and Patents Act 1988.

ISBN 978 1 84868 621 2

British Library Cataloguing in Publication Data.
A catalogue record for this book is available from
the British Library.

Typeset in 9.5pt on 12pt Celeste.
Typesetting by Amberley Publishing.
Printed in the UK.

Introduction

Dudley town grew up around The Ridgeway an ancient thoroughfare that crossed the countryside where Wolverhampton Street and Hall Street now run. We have no idea who the eponymous Dudda was who gave the name to the town, but the placename is derived from "Dudda's Woodland estate". After the Norman conquest of 1066 the lands around Dudelei were ceded to the Barons of Dudley who built a motte and bailey castle above the then village. It was Gervase Paganell and his ancestors who rebuilt the castle in stone and created the town to service its needs. By 1190 the town was known as Duddeleye, the Market Place in medieval times was surrounded by fields and still retains features of its agricultural past (see p. 24).

It was the development of the area's mineral resources during the Industrial Revolution that was to have a major impact on the town's fortunes. During the nineteenth century 'King Coal' and 'Prince Limestone' ruled. It was this exploitation of the area's geological heritage that caused much pollution and gave rise to the region being known as the Black Country. In Dudley, the population grew rapidly but the social conditions for most of the inhabitants of the town were not the best and disease was rife. This was remedied in the twentieth century with greatly needed slum clearance and the building of new houses (see p. 69).

The local government reorganisations of 1966 and 1974 meant that the borough had to merge with its neighbouring authorities. This brought about many changes in the resources available to the town. Significantly, but sometimes confusingly, the name of the new administrative area was kept, both times, as Dudley. This book deals solely with the pre 1966 borough.

In more recent memory the development of the Merry Hill Shopping Centre in Brierley Hill, commencing in 1985, saw the closure of department stores in the town centre. Marks & Spencer and Littlewoods moved out early on with Beatties (2010) being the latest to close. Boots happily survives. Nowadays the Market Place area is a shadow of its past but unexpectedly still attracts a number of shoppers. As for the future of the town, the Governments - Regional Spatial Strategy for the West Midlands cites Dudley as a "non-strategic town centre" but does see it as a "Black Country heritage attraction".

Photography has only been around since the mid nineteenth century; Fox Talbot did his pioneering work in the 1840s, so any reliable illustrations of the borough can only exist from that time onwards. Engraved images both on paper and metal are useful but the artist adapts the view to suit his needs and to add drama (see p. 7), this so called 'artistic licence' does not constitute reliable evidence. So, this then gives us a window of around two hundred years to look at a thousand years of development, albeit that the major changes to the town have occurred since about 1800.

Also, the artist or photographer is subjective in what they record; it is down to their whim, or their patrons, as to what they depict. Likewise the choice of what appears in this book depends on the available material and my preferences in selecting the illustrations. Hence this book, judged by these factors, is imperfect; still I hope you enjoy my choices which I trust will give the reader a taster of the character of my home town of Dudley.

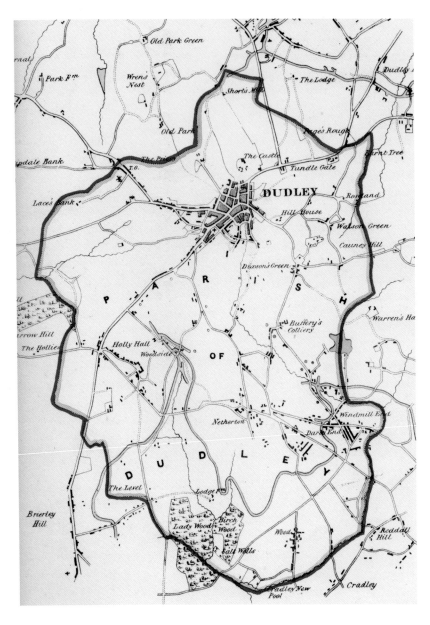

Map of Dudley
Borough *c.* 1840

ENTRANCE TO CASTLE GROUNDS, DUDLEY.

Entrance to Dudley Castle

For many years the citizens of Dudley and its neighbourhood enjoyed free access to the castle and its surrounding park. This all stopped in 1937 when the zoo was opened and the entrance moved further down Castle Hill. Many events including an annual fête were held in the castle courtyard. What is now The Fellows pub formed part of the gatehouse to the castle.

Castle Keep

There has been a castle on the hill overlooking Dudley for nearly a thousand years. Originally constructed of wood in 1070 the present stone keep was built in the thirteenth century. Occupied by the Royalists in the Civil War, the castle survived until 1750 when a fire gutted the complex. The token of 1797 shows the keep quite overgrown just before its transformation into the romantic ruin we see today.

Below – The reverse of the token states that it was issued by "E. Davies – Nail Factor". It is one of a series of four, the others being another view of the castle and two of the Priory, all issued at that date.

Overlooking the Black Country

This graphic from the *Illustrated London News* shows a rather fanciful nineteenth century view from the keep of Dudley Castle, as there is no earthbound way of having the tower of the keep in the foreground. The main thing to compare on these views is the background. Note the industrialisation that is polluting the area, hence 'Black Country' compared to the green space we see today.

Panorama of Dudley

What changes to the townscape of Dudley over 180 years! The top view was made about 1830 with some artistic licence. Note the spacing of St. Thomas's and St. Edmund's, 'Top' and 'Bottom', churches with St. Andrews, Netherton in the middle distance. Although the town has changed from a 'horse and cart' frame of mind to one dominated by the automobile, aspects of the old town remain constant. Note for example the Castle Street/Market Place and Tower Street thoroughfares.

Dudley in the Fifties

Although only taken in the 1950s the view shows off the 'developments' in Dudley during the past fifty years. Note the office block of Trident House dominating centre left, the loss of the Fire Station training tower, the growth of the Council House complex, the pylons of the lights on Stafford Street car park and the Butterfield Court tower block.

A Missed Opportunity

It is a pity that the photographer who took this picture in the 1950s of the view from the keep at Dudley Castle did not raise their camera a little to take in more of the vista, as the modern photograph does. Instead they have captured a family about to enter the triple gateway. Note the stairs for the elephant ride behind.

Zoo Entrance

Dudley Zoo opened to the public in 1937 and the first visitors, like so many after them, walked through these gates beneath the sweeping Tecton arches. Designed by Berthold Romanovich Lubetkin, a Russian émigré architect, these early modernist classic concrete arches have become an iconic symbol of the zoo and so deserve their Grade II* listing.

Looking down Castle Hill

Castle Hill has long been the main thoroughfare into Dudley and an entertainment centre for the town. One can see on the right the 1937 Odeon Cinema now partially obscured by the signboard, which became in 1976 a Jehovah's Witness Kingdom Hall. Other changes from the 1950s postcard include the Plaza being demolished in 1990.

Proprietor and Manager - J. MAURICE CLEMENT.

" I hold the world but as the world Gratiano."

" A Stage, where every man must play a part."

Merchant of Venice, Act I, Scene I.

Live Entertainment Venue

The Opera House was opened on Castle Hill on the 4 September 1899. It was founded, owned and managed by John Maurice Clement. The illustration is taken from a programme of 1901 advertising the theatre's Shakespearean season. Sadly the theatre caught fire in November 1936 but was immediately replaced by the Hippodrome. This continued to supply live entertainment until 1964, when it became a bingo hall. In the 1970s it was in part used as a nightclub but closed its doors in 2009.

13

Dudley Railway Station

Dudley Station opened in 1850 at the junction of the lines of the Oxford, Wolverhampton and Worcester Railway and the South Staffordshire Railway.

Later these were absorbed into the Great Western Railway and London & North Western Railways respectively with the latter being amalgamated into the London Midland & Scottish in 1923. The station remained in service until 1964 when it closed to passengers but was redeveloped three years later as a Freightliner Terminal, which carried on in use until 1986. After the closure of the Walsall—Stourbridge line in 1993 the track officially became mothballed awaiting the arrival of the Metro. Nature is now reclaiming the site but if you look clearly you can make out where the tracks still lie hidden.

The Station Hotels

Although Dudley Railway Station was opened in 1850 it would be nearly fifty years before the original Station Hotel was built on the corner of Birmingham Road and Trindle Road. Its owners, Wolverhampton and Dudley Breweries, demolished the old pub and rebuilt it in its current form in 1938. More recently it has gained a haunted reputation.

The Guest

Dudley Guest Hospital was originally opened in Tipton Road in 1861 as a Blind Asylum for the workers blinded or maimed in the local limestone mines. Following a bequest from Joseph Guest (hence the name change) it was reopened as a hospital in 1871. The new façade was added in the 1940s but sadly, following the extension of Russells Hall Hospital, the Guest closed in 2006 and the site now awaits its fate.

Guest Hospital, Dudley.

Looking up Castle Hill

Looking up Castle Hill from what is now called Castle Gate towards the town we have an interesting picture of the last days of the trams in Dudley. The time frame for this picture can be gained from the Hippodrome, in the centre of the picture, which is nearing completion prior to it opening, 19 December 1938. Trams stopped running from Dudley in September 1939. Annoyingly the building of the traffic island denies the prospect of seeing a bus come towards you.

View from Tipton Road

Dudley Cricket Ground was set up around 1865. It acquired the nickname 'County Ground' as Worcestershire CCC used to play some of their home matches here. Erosion of the limestone galleries beneath the pitch caused a major collapse on 25 May 1985 forcing the abandonment of the site. Following on from a major infilling exercise the site opened as Castle Gate Business Park in 1999. The Village Hotel and car park now occupy what was the County Ground.

Looking down Castle Street

In between the forty or so years that separate these two photographs many changes have been made to Castle Street. Firstly one cannot get the same viewpoint as a 'stylish' toilet block has been built to obstruct the view. The two pubs that feature in the foreground have changed use, the Hen & Chickens on the left closed in 1985 and is now a branch of Ladbrokes Bookmakers and the Angel, right middle, is now a British Heart Foundation charity shop.

Opening the Fountain

In 1867 the *Illustrated London News* reported on the opening of the new drinking fountain in Dudley. It was given as a gift from The Earl of Dudley and Ward to the "people of Dudley", in "order to encourage temperance", and was officially declared open by 'her Ladyship', Georgina, Countess of Dudley. It was designed by James Forsyth who was also responsible for the great Perseus Fountain at Witley Court, then the home of the Earl. In the 1980s, sometime after the water supply had been cut off, the bowls were filled in with concrete. However the Fountain still remains a major feature of the town and probably its most valuable piece of public sculpture.

Below right – Reverse of a commemorative medallion issued to mark the opening of the fountain showing the date of 17 October 1867, a Thursday.

People at the Fountain

Although about a hundred years separate these two photographs of the fountain in Dudley Market Place one thing remains constant; people are still using it as a meeting place. Most of the buildings in the older picture have long gone and the area has been pedestrianised, but note Boots the Chemist is in both photographs.

The Edwardian Market Place

Taken some time after 1905, little is left of buildings shown in this postcard of Dudley Market Place although clues are there. Look at the extreme left of each picture and you notice the edging stones of what is now River Island. The plain white building of the bank also retains its four second floor windows although the rest of the façade has been remodelled. Whoever coloured this originally black and white postcard could have done a better job.

Overview of the Market

The Market Place has been at the heart of Dudley for hundreds of years and still retains a link back to its origin. Note on the two photographs the sweep of the central aisle between the two rows of stalls this is not a regular curve but harks back to medieval times when it is said there was a spring flowing through the town centre and the market was set up on the banks either side of that watercourse.

Alan Price

The Railway Vaults
Its name dating from the opening of Dudley Railway Station in May 1850 and sited next to the Dudley Arms Hotel, the Railway Vaults originally only had a six day licence. This was increased to the full seven day licence in 1931. Closed in the early 1970s the building survived until 1984 when the whole block was demolished to make way for a new retail store. If you take a walk through the adjacent 'Long Entry' to King Street you will notice that it is curved which means it can trace its origins back to pre 1200 when the market area was fields and this thoroughfare was a trackway alongside a ditch.

Alan Price

The Dudley Arms Hotel

The Dudley Arms Hotel was built in the Market Place in 1786 on the site of a former inn. In the eighteenth and nineteenth centuries it was the principal posting house for the town handling fifteen to twenty coaches a day. It had stabling for thirty-two horses with its own blacksmith and wheelwright shops and sixteen bedrooms. The hotel was a cultural and social centre for the town. Amongst many things it was the headquarters of the Court Leet and on 15 August 1862 the Dudley Geological Society held its inaugural meeting here. Its demolition in 1968, just after this picture was taken, to make way for an extension to the adjacent Marks & Spencer store was an act of official vandalism on the town.

Hall Street/Market Place

Hall Street is an ancient thoroughfare in Dudley and contained some of its oldest buildings. Contrast the scene shown in the 1903 view to that of today. A lot of the change was caused by the Churchill Precinct development in the late 1960s which demolished a number of ancient shops and replaced them with a pedestrianised area. The Seven Stars Inn, one of the oldest inns in Dudley, closed its doors in 1960.

The Fountain Arcade

This advert taken from a local guidebook of 1929, just three years after the Fountain Arcade had opened, urges the reader to "watch our windows for novelties" and advertises a stock of "shelly china, cut glass, Worcester china, leather goods and fountain pens". Much has changed on the ground floor but the first floor looks fairly unaltered.

A Local Footballing Legend

Duncan Edwards was born in Dudley on 1 October 1936 and throughout his short life professed his pride in being an ambassador for the town. Duncan played his early football with Wolverhampton Street School and we see him surrounded by his school mates celebrating his England Youth call-up. However he will forever be associated with Manchester United and the so-called 'Busby Babes'. Twenty one year old Duncan actually survived the Munich air crash but died from horrific injuries nearly two weeks later on 21 February 1958. Duncan was buried in Dudley's Borough cemetery on Wednesday 26 February. Over 5,000 people stood in silence outside the Cemetery and lined the streets in tribute to the lad from Elm Road on the Priory Estate. On Thursday 14 October 1999 his mother, Mrs Sarah Edwards, and his former Manchester United colleague and friend, Sir Bobby Charlton, unveiled this statue commemorating the Dudley born footballer.

A Market Stall

There has been a market in Dudley since medieval times and I would guess that fruit and vegetables have always featured prominently. Many family 'dynasties' have had stalls on the market over the years including Brooke Bros., Southalls and Lampitts. It can be seen that in the intervening 100 years the variety of produce is similar but the dress of the stallholders, the market canopy and the prices have definitely altered.

Keith Hodgkins

29

Into the High Street I

Looking back towards the market we can see the changes and note the similarities in the fifty odd years between the two photographs. Barclays Bank still dominates the foreground but Wood's grocer, Hollywood Hats and Dudley's furnishing stores have long gone being replaced by Ethel Austin, the Co-op travel agency and the Abbey bank. This section of the High Street is closed to traffic on a Saturday.

Into the High Street II
This earlier view of the High Street, between 1900 and 1910, shows a long lost town centre. Most of the buildings have gone but the fountain remains a constant reference point. Note also the upper floors of Ryman Stationers, Halifax Bank and Thomas Cook travel agent still surviving from the houses built for William Bagott in 1840.

Dudley Building Society

Dudley and District Benefit Building Society was founded in 1858 and incorporated in 1895. In the early part of the twentieth century its address was 224 Market Place before moving to new premises in the Fountain Arcade. It is possibly here, in the 1940s, that the picture of the staff was taken, apparently the lady on the extreme right is Miss Evelyn Peacock. The newly named Dudley Building Society moved to its current location, in Stone Street, in the 1960s.

Alan Price

The Two Bulls Heads II
First recorded as the Bull's Head, Stone Street in 1819 the 'two' was added by the then licensee, Joseph Edwards, between 1871-1880. Still a busy market pub in 1968 when this picture was taken it was subsequently de-licensed in the mid 1980s and is now a temping agency.

Pub check/token issued by Joseph Edwards who was licensee between 1864 & 1884.

Stone Street Square

Stone Street Square has fulfilled many functions over the years including a market. The last trolley bus to Wolverhampton ran from here on the 5 March 1967 but no. 58 buses still ran from here for quite a few years after. Subsequently the site became a car park until following an archaeological investigation, which uncovered the Dudley Flint Glassworks of Abiather Hawkes, it was pedestrianised in 2001. It now hosts various events including this Police Family Fun Day in August 2009.

The Saracen's Head

First recorded in 1808 the Saracen's Head and Freemasons Arms, known locally as 'The Napper', dominates the corner of Stone Street and Priory Road. At one time it was a carriers house with stagecoach services departing every Saturday morning to Ludlow and Knighton going via Stourbridge, Kidderminster, Bewdley and Cleobury. Charles Ernest King was landlord 1922-27. Recently re-branded as 'The Source at the Saracens' we await the fate of this historic inn.

Brooke Robinson Museum

Brooke Robinson came from a family that had long been associated with Dudley. When he died in 1911 he bequeathed money to be used to build a museum. The legacy was used instead to provide the Town Hall complex, completed in 1931, with one room for the museum. This room, shown in the picture above, was isolated and so the collection was rarely viewed. In 1979 the Museum's Trustees agreed to the collection being moved to Dudley Museum and Art Gallery.

Dudley Library

The Right Hon. Georgina Countess of Dudley is seen here (centre picture) laying the foundation stone for Dudley Library, St. James's Road, on Friday 26 June 1908. Since the library opened, a year later, little has changed of the façade but inside it is a different matter, with numerous alterations being made to cater for the changing needs of us, the borrowers. The foundation stone can clearly be seen to right of the library entrance.

Civic Gardens

Originally laid out in 1939 these civic gardens opposite the Council House were, as the postcard from the 1940s below shows, named the Princess Gardens. Its name change to the Coronation Gardens came after the crowning of the former Princess Elizabeth in 1953. The piece of stone seen in the foreground was specially moved from Wren's Nest National Nature Reserve and bears a plaque commemorating the life of Bert Bissell, peace campaigner, 1902–1998.

Dudley Girls' High School

Dudley Girls' High School opened on this site in Priory Road in 1910 but could trace its origins back to 1881. It merged with the grammar school in 1975 and then with the Bluecoat School in 1989 to form the Castle High School. The school was eventually closed and subsequently demolished in 1996. Now serving as a car park the site has been sold and should soon see the building of an extension for Dudley College.

POLICE STATION DUDLEY.

Dudley's Police Stations

Built around 1847 Dudley's first police station, complete with lock up, was in Priory Street. These buildings served the town for nearly a hundred years until the new police station was built in New Street and opened by Lord Cobham on 22 October 1942. Originally it was planned to demolish the old buildings but the Second World War intervened and nowadays they form part of the council house complex.

'The Old Chestnut'

This view of Tower Street has achieved iconic status. It has probably been used in virtually every photographic book about Dudley and most about the Black Country but it is such a classic scene that it must be included here.

Little remains of the buildings shown on this early twentieth century postcard of Tower Street. All the buildings on the left disappeared with the road widening during the Second World War. The castle is the obvious reference point but also the railings for Baylies' Hall can be seen in the middle distance. The Malt Shovel Inn, next to the Hall, is known locally as 'The Mad House' and is notorious for a murder committed there in 1926.

Tower Street Corner

These two photographs of the junction of Tower Street with The Broadway are only about forty years apart but they serve to demonstrate the power of the automobile. These cottages which ooze rural charm were demolished in the early 1960s to make way for a car park.

Dudley Bus Station

Opened in 1952 Dudley Bus station, aka Fisher Street, has seen much use over the years as these photographs testify. The picture below was, judging from the clothing, taken in the late 1950s to 1960s. All was cleared away in 1985 for the development of a flatter bus station, made necessary by the number of accidents caused by brakes failing on buses parked on the slope. However St. Edmund's church and the castle still dominate the scene.

Looking at the Castle

This engraving entitled *Dudley Castle from the North East* dates from 1831. Step forward nearly a hundred and eighty years and compare it with a current view taken from a similar angle from the footbridge over the bypass. The rural scene has long gone and urbanisation rules.

Alan Price

King Street

These two views along King Street, looking towards the bus station, demonstrate the changes taken place in my home town of Dudley during the past fifty years. The Green Dragon pub on the corner of Flood Street closed in 1960 and was demolished soon after to make way for a car park. Note the two way dual carriageway system inanely put into place in the 1990s.

What's in a Name?

The Coach and Horses, first listed in 1830, was by the 1930s owned by Ansells Brewery and it was they who rebuilt the pub in 1936. In late 1987 the then owners changed its name to what was then its nickname, derived from the name of the lounge, 'The Old Vic'. The name was changed, yet again, in 1998 to 'Ye Olde Foundry'. It is the only pub still remaining in King Street.

Out of Austerity

This view of Wolverhampton Street from the late 1940s captures that period very well. The clothing of the people, the cars and even the scribbled note on the card all transport us back to that time of change. Much has altered over the ensuing years.

A Tale of Time
As the sign proudly
proclaims above their
shop in Wolverhampton
Street, John Hollins
has been trading as a
jeweller, and pawnbroker,
in Dudley since 1804.
Their other shop at
28 King Street closed
in the late 1950s and
was demolished soon
after to make way
for redevelopment.
The silver case which
contains the watch
movement depicted
is hallmarked for
Birmingham 1894.

Town Parades

Dudley town centre, in particular High Street, has long been the setting for numerous parades. This one, dating from the early 1900s, shows the thoroughfare packed with spectators watching the Mayor, with police escort, leading a procession of top hatted dignitaries through the town. The other shows the West Midlands Police Pipe Band leading the Remembrance Sunday Parade on 8 November 2009.

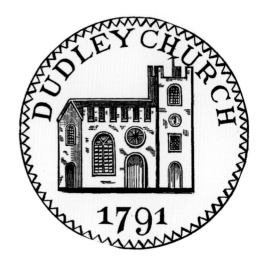

Top Church

Officially called the Parish Church of St. Thomas, this ecclesiastical building that dominates the views of Dudley is known locally as 'Top Church'. There has been a church recorded on the site since 1182, but by the time the vicar Dr. Luke Booker arrived in 1813 the building (see inset) was in a sorry state of repair. So in 1815 he obtained an Act of Parliament to demolish it and the foundation stone for the new church was laid, as the reverse of the medallion states, on the 25 October 1816. The legend on the medallion is in Greek and quotes Ephesians, chapter II, verse XX – "Jesus Christ himself being the first cornerstone". The church was opened on St. Thomas's Day, 21 December, 1818.

Above – Illustration of a pass, showing the old church, which was used to gain admission to the church yard on the day of the laying of the foundation stone that also entitled the bearer to buy a medallion.

The Gipsies Tent

Depicted at a book launch at the Priory Inn in 1989 are Don and Bert Millard the last licensees of the Gipsies Tent. They are seated either side of Frank Power a much respected local photographer. The Gipsies Tent stands on the junction of Steppingstone Street, Greystone Street and Stafford Street and was in the continual ownership of the Millard family from 1867 until it closure in 1980. The pub now stands empty and is gradually crumbling away.

Alan Price

Change of Use

There has been a public house at 21 Vicar Street since the 1860s although it was then called the Boilermakers Arms. The name change to the Locomotive Inn came in the 1890s. It closed as licensed premises on the 21 August 1973. Initially the building became the offices for G. Hill (Electrical Contractors) but now houses the Gurdwara Guru Teg Bahadur Sahib.

Alan Price

Along Hall Street

Captured in July 1968 the top photograph shows the row of small shops that stood in Hall Street before they were demolished in 1975 to make way for a Tesco supermarket that then became a Cousins superstore. One can make out the Empire Cinema at the end of the row at the junction with Dudley Row, just beyond there, on the photograph below, the low brick wall indicates that the Dudley Southern Bypass now runs beneath.

The Salvation Army

Founded in Dudley in 1877, the Salvation Army had its Citadel in King Street from 1912 until they sold these premises to Woolworths when they moved to their present premises in North Street. Dedicated on the 29 September 1975 it is built on the site of the former Christ Church Congregational Church in Hall Street. The Salvation Army in Dudley continues with its long tradition of bandsmanship.

Bean Cars

Between 1919 and 1926 Bean Cars were made in Dudley. To be precise the bodywork was made in Dudley but the chassis and engines were made in Tipton and then driven up to the Waddams Pool works for final assembly. After the Dudley site was sold off in 1926 all work transferred to Tipton, with car production ceasing in 1929 and commercial vehicles in 1931. The Bean Cars sign can still be seen above the former offices.

Dixon's Green Methodist Church

Dixon's Green Methodist Church was originally opened in 1870 and the top picture shows how it looked in 1902, however it was 'modernised' with a front extension and new façade in 1950. Although the manse next door is now in a state of disrepair the chapel is still in regular use.

Free No More
Located at 69, St. John's Road, Kate's Hill is the Freebodies Tavern. There has been a licensed premise on this site since about the 1830s. William Whitehouse brewed here between 1888 and 1906. The old pub was demolished and the present one rebuilt in 1976. It was then refurbished and reopened on 26 January 2004. Sadly since this time, like so many local pubs, the Freebodies fell into disuse and has become a target for vandalism; a sorry state of affairs.

Kate's Hill School

Pupils of the top year at Kate's Hill Junior School are seen here with their teacher, Mr Ron Willets, on a visit to Dudley Zoo in early 1960 (author is shown top left). The old Kate's Hill Infant and Junior Schools which were sited on the junction of Owen Street and St. Johns Street sadly caught fire during half term holiday in May 1969 and were later demolished. The new Primary and Nursery schools opened on their site in Peel Street in 1972/3.

From Leafy Lane

Dixon's Green has long been a major thoroughfare into Dudley from Rowley and Blackheath although things have changed somewhat in the century between these views. No longer a leafy backwater with residences for prosperous shopkeepers and tradesmen the road, now designated as the B4171, has become a busy highway.

Dixons Green, Dudley.

Old Post Office

Erected in 1909, at the junction of Priory Street and Wolverhampton Street, Dudley's main post office had a long and illustrious career and several facelifts until its closure in 1988. The business was transferred to 237-8 High Street but was then sub-contracted out in 2007 and is now part of the Safeway supermarket at the junction of High Street and Union Street. The old building at first became a nightclub but now stands disused.

Dudley Old Bank

Dudley Old Bank was originally built in 1791 and was then eventually taken over by Lloyds Banking Group in 1866 who demolished the original building and built the new bank in 1876. Things then remained rather stable, in banking terms, until the late twentieth century when we had the merger of Lloyds with TSB to form a 'super bank' leading to the eventual closure of the branch in 2005.

Wolverhampton Street I

Looking towards the town centre we see the changes that have taken place over around a hundred years. In the first photograph we see the street decked out to celebrate some national event whereas the modern photograph sees the view from the top of a double-decker bus. The Crown public house closed in 1996 but has since seen life as a fish and chip restaurant and two different wine bars before again becoming vacant. It is currently, January 2010, being refurbished by Dudley MBC.

Keith Hodgkins

Wolverhampton Street II

Contrast these two views of Wolverhampton Street, looking towards Eve Hill. The buildings in the foreground seem little altered but those further on have changed somewhat. Dominating the left foreground is Finch House, or 29-30 Wolverhampton Street, this simple classical house has a date stone of 1707 and was built for Joseph and Mary Finch. The Finch family were nail ironmongers and merchants who had a long history of non-conformity.

Above – Obverse of a farthing (0.1p) token issued by John Finch, an ancestor of Joseph and Mary, in about 1665.

Wesley Methodist Chapel

Dudley has always had a strong link with non-conformists, at one point there being over twenty chapels in the Borough. The Wesley Methodist in Wolverhampton Street, was the second oldest in Dudley, founded in 1829 it held its last service on 28 October 1973. It being then demolished and replaced by the new Central Methodist Church which opened in 1978.

WILLIAM DOVEY,
Cart, Van and Wagon Builder,

HORSES CAREFULLY SHOD.

Wheels New Tyred, and all kinds of Smiths' Work done on the Premises.

28 & 29, SOUTHALLS LANE, DUDLEY.

28 Southalls Lane

This advert that appeared in various local directories at the beginning of the twentieth century demonstrates how what we now call rural crafts were then part and parcel of everyday life. Number 28 Southalls Lane is now occupied by Arthur Ashmore (Tailors) Ltd. who specialise in gentlemen's attire for ballroom dancers.

Dudley Grammar School

Dudley Grammar School was founded in about 1562 but did not move to the St. James's Road site until 1899. Since that time there have been various extensions to the buildings, none more so than in preparation for its amalgamation with the Dudley Girls High School and Bluecoat School to form Castle High School in 1989.

Dudley Cluniac Priory

Dudley Priory was founded by Gervase Pagnel in about 1160 at the behest of his father Ralph, and was affiliated to Wenlock Abbey. Judging from its size there would probably not have been more than six Cluniac monks there at any one time. Following the dissolution of the monasteries by Henry VIII in 1538, like so many other places of worship, it fell into disrepair. Comparing the engraving of *c.* 1775 to the photograph today shows the process is continuing.

Priory Hall

To celebrate the incorporation, under Royal Charter, of Dudley as a Borough in 1865 Mr Frederick Smith, the first Mayor, threw the grounds of his house, Priory Hall, open to the school children of Dudley. On the 29 August some 4000 pupils, together with their teachers, descended upon the grounds to "partake of tea and plumcake and to enjoy games of various kinds". Mr Smith was also the Mines Agent for the Earl of Dudley. The grounds were opened as a public park in July 1932 and the Grade II listed Hall, built in 1825, is now the home of the Dudley Registration & Celebratory Services.

A View over the Priory

Here again we can see how the rural feel of Dudley has been eaten away. Contrast the top photograph of the farm buildings surrounding Priory Hall, taken before 1930, with the current view which shows the two thousand houses which were built on the Priory Estate during that decade. The Technical College, sitting below the castle, was built in 1936.

Seven Sisters Caverns

The Seven Sisters caverns are seen depicted in an engraving of 1831. These vast caverns were hewn out by miners seeking the limestone that makes up the bulk of Wren's Nest. Sadly the Seven Sisters were infilled in 2003, as a holding exercise until such time as funding is available to bring these caves back to their former glory. The architect's image is based on a laser survey of the inside of the cavern.

New photograph courtesy Dudley MBC, impressions by Knight Architects with Moxon Architects.

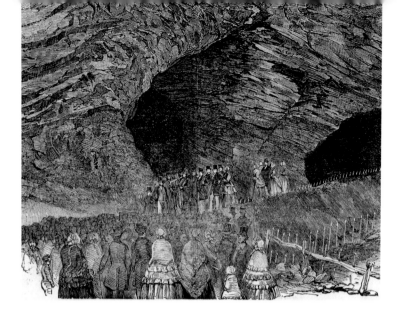

Murchisson Revisited

This engraving of 1849 shows Sir Roderick Murchisson delivering his address to members of the British Association, on Saturday 15 inst, in the caverns below Dudley Castle. The newspaper reported that "nearly 15000 people availed themselves of the privilege during the day". Sir Roderick had the nickname of 'Mr Siluria' as he had the distinction of being the scientist who defined the Geological time period of the Silurian Age primarily from the fossils discovered beneath the Wren's Nest. On 27 September 2006 part of the International Conference to celebrate the 50th Anniversary of Wren's Nest becoming the first urban National Nature Reserve for Geology there was an evening canal trip into the caverns beneath Castle Hill. A number of us decided to commemorate Murchission's visit by donning Victorian attire.

Top left to right – Sebastian Haywood, David Hill, Trevor Conroy, Peter Glews, Adrian Durkin and Robert Earnshaw. Bottom left to right – Penny Russell, Kevin Clements, Nicola Havers, Anna Coward, Lesley Gorski, Graham Worton, Sarah Worton, Alan Cutler.

HILLY HOUSE, LONDON FIELD'S, Nr DUDLEY
BOWLING GREEN - Good ALES
PROPRIETOR, R. CARDO. - 1914

Hilly Houses

An inn since 1873, the Hilly House was originally at 11 Corser Street but the licence was transferred to its present site on Himley Road, a stones throw away, in December 1955. It is perhaps ironic that the last owner of the premises before it became a pub was a staunch teetotaller. Richard Cardo, who was licensee 1911–1920, would no doubt have been proud that the Hilly House still has a strong bowling tradition, fielding teams in numerous local divisions.

Ron Moss collection

Russells Hall Blast Furnaces

Russells Hall Blast furnaces had a very short life only existing between 1827 and 1869. The earliest furnaces are the second and third from the right with the newest one on the far right. They stood beside an ancient trackway that linked Russell Hall on the Himley Road and Scotts Green. This now terminates at the gate opposite 25/25a Russells Hall Road, by the lamppost centre picture, which in turn now occupy part of the site of the furnaces.

Plumes of Feathers

The Plume of Feathers originally stood at 148 Upper High on what was known as 'the Highside', about opposite what is now Derann's store. Nestled in next to the Black Horse Inn, it has been recorded as a licensed premise since the 1790s and was the last 'home brew' pub in Dudley town centre when it stopped in 1955. An explosion in the cellar on 30 December 1961, rendered the building unsafe and it was demolished. The licence was transferred, in 1967, to the newly built estate pub on Russells Hall, at the junction of Russells Hall Road and Overfield Road. Despite various refurbishments it is now, in early 2010, being converted to a Co-op store.

Above – example of a pub check/token issued by Ezekiel Allen who was landlord between 1879 and 1888.

Making a Splash

Originally in New Mill Street Dudley Baths was, literally, a place where the local Victorians who had little in the way of sanitation, could go to have a bath. Later on the baths moved to Blowers Green Road and included areas for public swimming but had separate male and female pools. In September 1929 the new baths, shown, were opened adjacent to the old pools. The complex survived until 1976. Dudley Leisure Centre was opened in November 1978 in Wellington Road.

Higher Grade School I
The foundation stone for the St. Thomas's Old School, King Street, latterly the Higher Grade School, was laid on 25 March 1847. Closing as a school in 1970 it then became for many years a Pathfinder menswear store. This was often used as a reference to give directions to JB's which was located next door. Since the Pathfinder closed in 1993 the building has had many uses including an antiques shop until becoming the Mat de Mandir temple.

Higher Grade School II

Higher Grade Schools were a feature of the education system between 1876 and 1902. They took the better achieving pupils from the local secondary schools and educated them in science and technical subjects. Dudley's Parish Church Higher Grade school was attached to St. Thomas's Church in King Street. The pupils in the photograph are gathered around the entrance steps to the former church hall which can be seen clearly in the centre of the picture below.

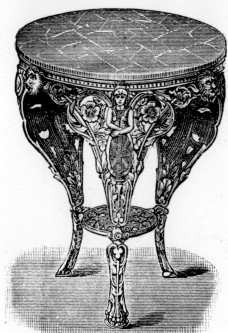

SMITH & DAVIES,

Established 1795.

General Ironfounders

AND

ART METAL WORKERS,

Manufacturers of Berlin, Black
and Brass Fenders, Kerbs and
Fire Dogs, Brass Kerbs, Fenders
and Umbrella Stands, Cast-iron
ROUND & OBLONG TABLES,
Garden Seats, Kitchen Oven
Grates, Boilers, Doors, Frames
and Bars. Spouting and Rain-
water Pipes.

KING STREET FOUNDRY

DUDLEY.

A Patriotic Table

Smith & Davies's factory was on
the corner of King Street and
Churchfield Street, a site until
recently occupied by Kwik Fit
Tyres. The table featured in their
1909 advert appears to have a
marble top whereas the one
pictured in the Lamp Tavern,
some 200m away from the site
of the factory, has a wooden
top, possibly a replacement. It is
interesting to contemplate the
history of the table in the Lamp
and wonder if it has travelled
less than a quarter of a mile
in its lifetime. Unfortunately
nothing can be proved either
way but it makes a good story.

Alan Price

At Queens Cross

Much has changed to the surrounds of the Lamp Tavern and its Bathams beer during the forty years that separate these photographs. Looking down Blower's Green Road from Queens Cross, the houses on the corner have disappeared, opening up the vista to the old Queen's Cross Brewery built *c.* 1870 which last brewed in 1934. This building was at the time of the earlier photograph home to Dudley Judo Club but now serves as a function room for the pub.

A Much Named School

Opened as the Upper Standard School in 1904, it became the Higher Elementary School in 1912 and the Intermediate School in 1929. It has always been a secondary school providing education to children over eleven mainly in modern and practical subjects. On gaining grammar school status in 1957 its name was changed, again, to the Sir Gilbert Claughton School. Closing as a school in 1990 it is now primarily used as council offices with the old school hall being a community centre.

The Mortuary Chapel

This image of the Mortuary Chapel at Dudley Cemetery, at Springs Mire, was made about the time of the cemetery's official opening on 30 September 1903. It replaced an earlier cemetery just up the road on Farthings Field. Note the Chapel has two entrances to cater for both Church of England and non-conformist religions. The thirty acre site still remains the only public burial site in the old Borough.

The Church, Hollyhall near Dudley

Holly Hall I

Looking towards Dudley from Holly Hall in about 1900 one would have had the view shown in the top postcard. St. Augustine's church was completed in 1884 and the fountain on the right was erected to commemorate the wife of Brooke Robinson, for many years MP for Dudley, after she died in 1892. The Holly Hall fountain was removed in 1954 on the grounds that it confused pedestrians trying to cross the road.

Holly Hall II

This vista from Holly Hall looking towards Merry Hill, down Pedmore Road, looked very different a hundred years ago as the top postcard testifies. The Holly Hall Schools were built by Alexander Brodie Cochrane, the proprietor of the once famous Woodside iron, steel and engineering works, in 1860 for the children of the workers. When the works closed, in 1921, the schools then enjoyed the patronage of the Earl of Dudley.

GENERAL VIEW
COCHRANE & CO (WOODSIDE) LTD. DUDLEY.
PURCHASED BY JOHN CASHMORE. AUGUST 1924.

Cochrane's Legacy

Nothing now remains of the site of Cochrane & Co. Ironworks in Woodside. The local housing estate, which covers the former works, has a Cochrane Road as gesture to this major institution. To my mind however this factory's legacy lives on in examples of their output in the form of pillar boxes still being used at the Black Country Living Museum, St. Fagans, National History Museum, Cardiff, Liverpool Docks, Matlock and Gosport to name but a few locations. Over a hundred years after they were made. The Woodside Iron Works was also associated with many important structures, including Westminster Bridge, Charing Cross Railway Bridge and Station, and the Runcorn Bridge over the Mersey. They also removed the Hungerford Suspension Bridge over the Thames and re-erected it as the Clifton Suspension Bridge at Bristol. The works closed in 1921 but carried on as John Cashmores Ltd. until 1939.

Below – Makers plate on the railway bridge at Liverpool Road Station, now part of Manchester Science Museum.

Towards Netherton

Cinder Bank has always been part of the main thoroughfare between Dudley and Netherton though how it got its more industrial sounding name is a mystery. Considerable road widening has gone on, to the right, since the picture was taken in 1905 although the houses to the left remain much the same.

Netherton High Street
Over the ensuing century that has passed between these two views of Netherton High Street, looking towards Dudley, the buildings have changed but some still retain their character. However the major change must be the traffic! Somewhat ironically Netherton is the Anglo-Saxon for lower farm.

Halesowen Road

These two pictures, some hundred years apart, show the changes in Halesowen Road, Netherton, looking towards Old Hill. The Church of England School, on the right, is now a Furniture Warehouse and further down the Junction Inn now a centre for Help the Aged. However the window layout of the first floor of the building now occupied by Taylor Made Specs and Bains Wines remains constant.

Halesowen Road Reversed

Looking up the road to Dudley we see Plants Steam Brewery the white structure, in the centre distance, so this dates this picture to pre 1912. It was then that this brewery, founded in 1837, was taken over and closed. The Mash Tun pub was latterly built on the site until that in turn was demolished in 1999 to make way for flats. The buildings on the right are still recognisable and the Old Swan Inn (Mrs Pardoes) is clearly marked.

A House Collapse

At about 1.40 am on Tuesday 29 August 1905, a house on Halesowen Road, Netherton suddenly collapsed. The cause of the subsidence was blamed on mining operations. Richard Hughes (twenty-two) was asleep in bed on the first floor at that time and although he was dug out of the wreckage unharmed, he sadly died of pneumonia, caused by shock and exposure, a few days later. Note the window details of the Junction Inn on the right of the postcard.

Church Road

Looking down Church Road, Netherton towards the town centre it would seem little has changed in the eighty or so years that separate these two photographs. Trinity Methodist Chapel on the right still features prominently and the houses seem little altered, the street lamps have changed and bus stops have appeared.

Where's the Fountain?

Netherton Park is located on the former wastes of Netherton Colliery, these were drained and landscaped in 1901, about the time this postcard was issued. The current location of the drinking fountain, which previously stood on the junction of Halesowen Road and Cradley Road is currently unknown.

Fountain, Netherton Park.

198-11.

Noah Hingley's

Founded in 1838 the Netherton firm of Noah Hingley and Sons Ltd. became world famous for their skill in making chain. Perhaps their most celebrated order was taken in 1911 for the RMS *Titanic*, although they did make chain for numerous other ships during their long history. The first picture is a view across the canal of the main Primrose Hill works taken in their heyday, probably during the 1930s. These works were demolished following the closure of the firm in 1969 and replaced by the Trading Estate we see today. The kink in the canal gives a reference point.

Netherton Furnaces

First recorded about 1817, by 1839 these furnaces were owned by the New Brtish Iron Company. Between 1858 and 1873 they were owned by of Noah Hingley & Co. Joseph H. Pearson, who issued the postcard, had title to the site from 1873 to 1913, it then came under the control of Baldwins who continued in business until 1925. The works were then dismantled by Thomas W. Ward between 1928 and 1930. The site is now occupied by the houses of Chichester Avenue but the Rowley Hills can still clearly be seen in the background.

Below – Obverse of a farthing (0.1p) token issued by S. M. Wright a "Tea Dealer, Grocer & Provision Merchant" in about 1845, whose business was in Netherton.

The Sounding Bridge, Netherton

53026. JV.

The Sounding Bridge

Spanning the Dudley No. 2 canal, the Sounding Bridge, or Highbridge Road Bridge, was built in the 1850s to replace a short tunnel known as Brewin's Tunnel (named after Thomas Brewin an engineer on the canal). Commercial traffic is now long gone from the canal but it still has a role for recreation. Netherton Reservoir is just to the left of this view.

Acknowledgements

I am indebted to numerous people I have met over my many years of collecting who have shared their knowledge with me. It has been that foundation that this volume has been built on. In particular I must mention Keith Hodgkins who put me forward for this tome and has been my main proof reader and consultant. My colleagues from Dudley MBC have kindly allowed me to use several images, Penny and Nicola have also helped with proof reading, and John Hemingway has been my historical advisor, thanks. Alan Price took many photographs around the Black Country in the 1960s and his shots of Dudley are classics; it was a privilege to have access to his archive. Last but not least Ron Moss has been studying the Industrial Archaeology of the Black Country, in particular chain making, for many years and for his guidance over many years I am thankful.

Unless otherwise specified all photographs are by the author and all items from the author's collection.

Forged Dudley Old Bank banknote of 1810 for five pounds (see p. 61) most probably made by the infamous William Booth of Perry Barr.

Bibliography

Title	Author	Publisher	Year
Dudley in Old Photographs	H. Atkins, D, Matthews & S. Robins	Sutton	1998
Dudley – The Twentieth Century	H. Atkins, D, Matthews & S. Robins	Sutton	1999
The Blackcountryman - Various	The Black Country Society		
Blocksidges Almanacks 1881-1950	E. Blocksidge	Blocksidge	1881 -1950
Dudley Castle and Priory	E. Blocksidge	Blocksidge	1906
Brochure of Dudley Castle Fête & Historical Pagent	E. Blocksidge	Blocksidge	1908
Dudley – As it was and is Today	G. Chandler & I. C. Hannah	Batsford	1949
The Curiosities of Dudley and the Black Country	C. F. G. Clark	Buckler Brothers	1881
Dudley Herald Yearbook 1903-1912	Dudley Herald		1903-1912
Inns' and 'Inn Signs' of Dudley	Mark H. Washington Fletcher	J. P.	1952
The Black Country Iron Industry	W. K. V. Gale	The Metals Society	1979
The Standard Catalogue of Provincial Banks and Banknotes	G. L. Grant	Spink	1977
The Illustrated Chronicle of Dudley Town and Manor	John Hemingway	MFH Publishing	2009
The Illustrated Chronicle of Dudley Castle & Barony 1070 - 1757	John Hemingway		2006
The Illustrated Chronicle of the Cluniac Priory of St. James, Dudley	John Hemingway	Friends of Priory Park	2005
Hitchmoughs Black Country Pubs – Dudley (CD)	Tony Hitchmough	Longpull	2007
Dudley Tradesmen Tokens	H. Perkins	Blocksidge	1905
Dudley in Old Picture Cards	David F. Radmore	European Library	1985
The Pubs & Breweries of the Old Dudley Borough	John Richards	Real Ale Books	1989
Black Country Tramways	J. S. Webb	Copperfield	1976
Black Country Chapels	Ned Williams	Sutton	2004
Dudley Rediscovered	Ned Williams	Uralia Press	2008
Netherton in Old Photographs	Ned Williams	Sutton	2006